# THE SOMME

## John Laffin

### Illustrations by Errol Nathaniel

Kangaroo Press

In this book, you will read a lot about divisions, brigades and battalions. This can be confusing, but below you can see how the Australian Imperial Force was organised. There were five divisions made up of three brigades each. Each brigade consisted of four battalions. Most battalions were entirely made up of soldiers from one or other of the states of Australia. Smaller subdivisions included companies, platoons and sections.

Officially, a division consisted of 18 000 men and a battalion of about 1000. The number of men available to fight, however, was often much fewer than this.

At the end of the book, there is a glossary where some other military words are explained.

## AIF FORMATION

### FIRST DIVISION

| 1st BRIGADE | 2nd BRIGADE | 3rd BRIGADE |
|---|---|---|
| 1 Battalion | 5 Battalion | 9 Battalion |
| 2 Battalion | 6 Battalion | 10 Battalion |
| 3 Battalion | 7 Battalion | 11 Battalion |
| 4 Battalion | 8 Battalion | 12 Battalion |

### SECOND DIVISION

| 5th BRIGADE | 6th BRIGADE | 7th BRIGADE |
|---|---|---|
| 17 Battalion | 21 Battalion | 25 Battalion |
| 18 Battalion | 22 Battalion | 26 Battalion |
| 19 Battalion | 23 Battalion | 27 Battalion |
| 20 Battalion | 24 Battalion | 28 Battalion |

### THIRD DIVISION

| 9th BRIGADE | 10th BRIGADE | 11th BRIGADE |
|---|---|---|
| 33 Battalion | 37 Battalion | 41 Battalion |
| 34 Battalion | 38 Battalion | 42 Battalion |
| 35 Battalion | 39 Battalion | 43 Battalion |
| 36 Battalion | 40 Battalion | 44 Battalion |

### FOURTH DIVISION

| 4th BRIGADE | 12th BRIGADE | 13th BRIGADE |
|---|---|---|
| 13 Battalion | 45 Battalion | 49 Battalion |
| 14 Battalion | 46 Battalion | 50 Battalion |
| 15 Battalion | 47 Battalion | 51 Battalion |
| 16 Battalion | 48 Battalion | 52 Battalion |

### FIFTH DIVISION

| 14th BRIGADE | 15th BRIGADE | 8th BRIGADE |
|---|---|---|
| 53 Battalion | 57 Battalion | 29 Battalion |
| 54 Battalion | 58 Battalion | 30 Battalion |
| 55 Battalion | 59 Battalion | 31 Battalion |
| 56 Battalion | 60 Battalion | 32 Battalion |

### 'THE SOMME?' WHAT DOES THAT MEAN?

Mention 'the Somme' to many Australians today and they will look mystified, and understandably so. Also, a reference to 'The Battle of the Somme' leaves them puzzled. So, what and where was the Somme?

The Somme looms large in Australia's history because it was Australia's most costly battle of World War I. Thousands of Australian soldiers lost their lives during the two battles of the Somme. Many more were maimed, blinded or gassed.

The Somme is the name of a river in France. It is also the name given to the region that surrounds the river. The Somme was not the only place where Australians fought during the war – Gallipoli, in Turkey, is the most famous of Australia's battlefields and the Australian Imperial Force (AIF) served in other parts of France, Belgium and the Middle East with distinction.

Using the word 'battle' to describe the fighting along the line of the Somme is misleading. Most people think of a battle as lasting a short time. The Battle of Waterloo in 1815 was over in a day; even the Battle of El Alamein in October 1942 lasted only nine days. The operations in the Somme lasted for many months and were really a campaign made up of many battles. The First Battle of the Somme was one of the most prolonged military agonies in history and it was waged over three seasons — summer, autumn and winter.

The AIF fought two battles of the Somme. The first lasted from 1 July until 18 November 1916; the second was fought between 21 March and late August 1918. These dates, however, do not take into account the many battles that took place north and south of the Somme between and after the two great battles. Australians were fighting in the area almost until the end of the war in November 1918.

In 1916, the Somme was a killing field. Many of its place names have become famous and infamous in Australian military history: famous for heroic endeavour and stubborn fortitude, infamous for slaughter, suffering and inept leadership

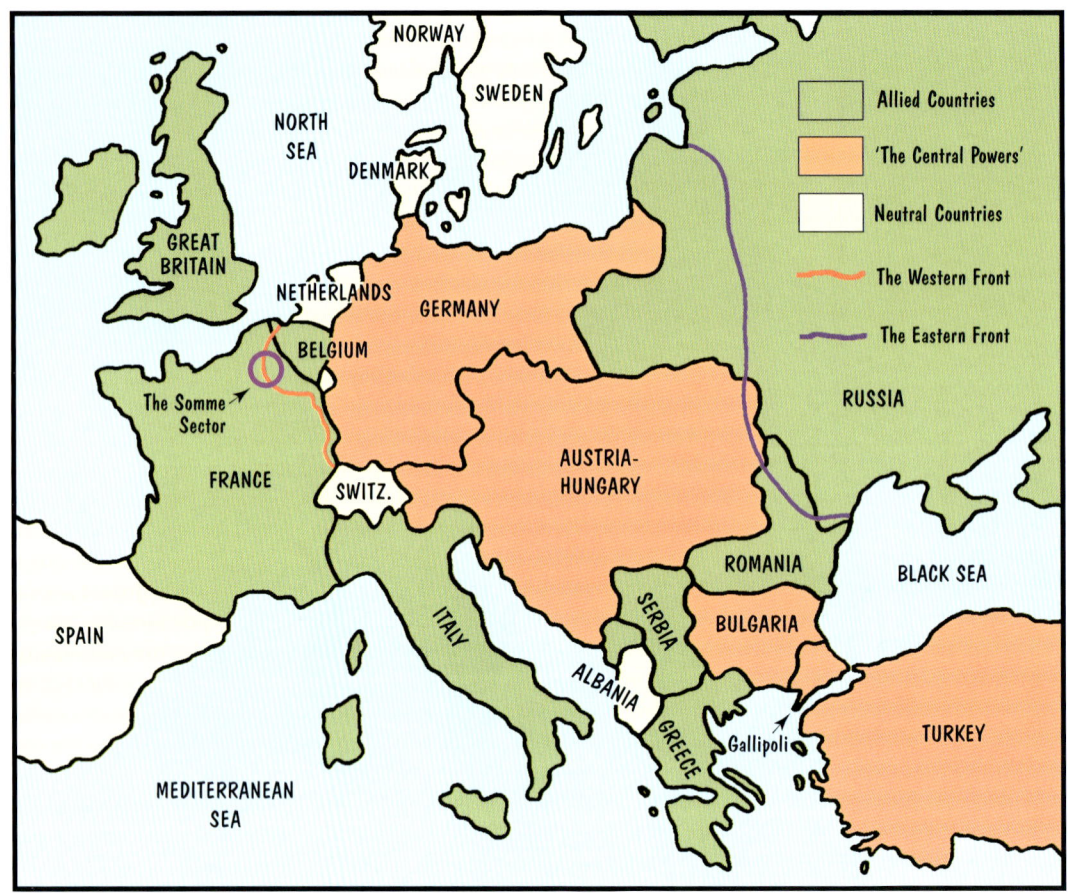

This map shows the situation in Europe in the summer of 1917, just after Italy joined the Allies and a few months before the war ended on the Eastern Front.

### THE ROAD TO THE SOMME: 'PLENTY OF BLOOD TO GO AROUND'

At the start of the twentieth century Europe had been at peace for the best part of one hundred years. However there were increasing tensions between the major powers over regional rivalries and old wrongs to be avenged. Nations competed to have the most powerful armies and the largest fleets. Complex alliances had also been formed where one country promised to help another if it was attacked. It was a very dangerous situation because a dispute between two countries could easily lead to a catastrophic war between the two great alliances: Britain, France and Russia on one side versus Germany and Austria–Hungary on the other.

There was no single cause of World War I, but the spark that started it was the assassination in June 1914 of the heir to the throne of the Austria–Hungarian Empire — the Archduke Ferdinand — by a Serbian student. The resulting dispute between Austria–Hungary and Serbia resulted in all the major powers preparing for war. Within days, Germany launched a military operation that had long been planned for such circumstances. Believing that attack was the best form of defence, the German army swept through Belgium and came very close to Paris before the French, British and Belgian armies forced the German army back north.

It quickly became clear that neither side was going to defeat the other easily. Modern defensive artillery and machine-gun fire left each side no choice but to dig into the ground for cover. The line where the armies dug in became known as the Western Front (there was also an Eastern Front on the other side of Europe where the Germans fought the Russians).

The Western Front stretched for nearly 800 kilometres from the edge of the North Sea in Belgium to the

Eager troops bound for the Somme bid farewell to Australia in July 1916.

border of France and Switzerland. The opposing armies dug thousands of kilometres of trenches, which they protected with artillery, machine-guns and masses of barbed wire. Often these trenches were only metres apart and troops could easily see the faces of the enemy and hear them talking.

During 1914 and 1915, the opposing armies suffered colossal casualties as thousands of men were ordered to charge at the enemy's trenches into machine-gun fire and exploding shells. Time and time again these tactics failed, but the generals seemed to learn nothing from the losses.

British divisions then serving abroad were rushed home and Canadian and Indian divisions were thrown into what some worried people were calling 'the meat grinder'.

No wonder then that the British generals were keenly interested in reinforcing their depleted and exhausted armies on the killing fields with fresh and eager Australian troops. Only two divisions of them and one of New Zealanders were available at that time, but more were coming.

\* \* \*

Australia, as a self-governing Dominion of Great Britain, was automatically at war when Great Britain declared war on Germany. Even though the war could hardly have been further away, most Australians thought of Britain as 'Home' and almost nobody questioned that Britain's war was Australia's war as well. Thousands of men volunteered, some out of a sense of duty and anger at what Germany had done, while many more were simply hoping for an exciting adventure.

When the Australian Imperial Force left home in 1914 for war service overseas, the soldiers were first landed in Egypt to help protect the Suez Canal, the vital waterway which led to India, the Far East and Australia. A new threat then developed when Turkey sided with Germany and Austria–Hungary. In an attempt to attack Germany and Austria–Hungary from the rear, Australian and New Zealand troops, along with British and French, were sent to capture the Dardanelles, the Turkish straits which opened the way to the Black Sea and Russia. This was the Gallipoli campaign, which brought the great story of the Anzacs (Australian and New Zealand Army Corps) into Australian history.

The Gallipoli campaign ended in failure and the withdrawal in December 1915 of the Australians and New Zealanders to Egypt, where they resumed training.

The Anzacs were in no way disgraced by the Gallipoli defeat. The failure was one of leadership, not of soldierly skill, and the Australians left Gallipoli with a tremendous reputation as fighting men.

The War Council and the High Command of the British Army were interested in the future of the AIF. Some British generals considered the Australians to be undisciplined, but all agreed that they had great 'potential'. Soon the order was given and the Australians filed onto troopships and sailed for the Western Front.

When they first reached France, these eager and enthusiastic men were disappointed when their units were sent not into battle, but to 'the Nursery', where reinforcements were trained. Here they endured boring lectures on subjects such as bathing and disinfection in military baths — which were usually in the great vats of breweries and bakeries. Similarly, they were taught how to prevent frostbite and the correct method of relieving a trench garrison. More to their satisfaction, many officers and selected men were sent to army schools to learn about trench-mortars, sniping and bombing.

While the Australians were training for the battles to follow, General Sir Douglas Haig, the new Commander-in-Chief of the British and Imperial Armies, was planning a great offensive over the rolling countryside north of the River Somme, which was to begin on 1 July 1916.

His strategy was straightforward attrition. This meant that if he could kill more Germans than they could kill British troops, victory would be his — or so he believed.

One of the many posters produced urging eligible men to join the forces. The AIF was the only completely volunteer army serving on the Western Front, but there was tremendous pressure to enlist. Young men who stayed at home were often accused of being cowardly and selfish.

But on the other side of no-man's-land the Germans held the high ground everywhere and they had made intelligent use of it. Thousands of their machine-guns covered every possible approach. Their field artillery and heavy guns were precisely ranged on the approaches across no-man's-land and on the positions that the attackers would occupy, if they could.

The AIF played no part in the first three weeks of the battle of the Somme but some British soldiers 'comforted' them with the grim assurance, 'Don't worry, Aussie, there's plenty of blood to go around.' And they meant British and Empire blood, not that of the enemy.

Elsewhere much of the spilled blood belonged to Australians. An example of just how great a blood sacrifice was required became apparent to the Diggers during the Battle of Fromelles, near the French–Belgian border, on 19–20 July 1916. The 5th Division, in conjunction with a British division, was called upon to capture the enemy positions near the village of Fromelles, where the Germans had already beaten back two Allied assaults. The defeated British commander, General Sir Richard Haking, planned the latest attack and yet again he sent his men in during broad daylight, without any attempt at surprise.

The 5th Division took and held some enemy trenches but it was impossible to reinforce the men or to resupply them. In 29 hours of fighting, the 5th Division suffered 5339 casualties. Senior Australian commanders tried to warn General 'the Butcher' Haking that the attack could not succeed, but he refused to listen. The men displayed remarkable heroism and determination, but no amount of courage could succeed against massed machine-gun fire. Details of the terrible loss were kept from the Australian soldiers then moving south towards the Somme.

## AND INTO BATTLE

The First Battle of the Somme began on 1 July 1916, with the British attacking on a front of 30 kilometres. Their generals told the troops that after a tremendous four-day bombardment of the enemy defences, they would merely have to 'stroll across' and occupy the German trenches. It was certainly not like that and the first day saw one of the worst disasters in any war.

The Germans had better trenches than the Allies and were able to weather the storm of exploding shells in their deep dugouts lined with reinforced concrete. When the British barrage eased, they ran to their posts with their deadly Maxim machine-guns. Using these guns and with rifle fire, they killed 21 000 British soldiers and wounded another 40 000 in a matter of hours. At Beaumont Hamel, the Newfoundland Regiment was annihilated almost to a man, as they advanced slowly across open country. Many Germans stood upright or knelt on their parapets to get a better aim at the heavily equipped and slow-moving enemy.

At first the German soldiers did not fully comprehend what was happening — it all seemed so easy. One officer later wrote, 'The British soldiers all lay down.' He and others thought that the 'Tommies' were doing this for protection. It took the Germans a while to understand the immense scale of their slaughter.

By the time the Australians reached the back areas they heard many rumours about atrocious fighting in hellish conditions. One was that the life expectancy of a young officer was no more than 24 hours. This was true. Another rumour was that the German soldiers could throw their 'stick' and 'egg' grenades further than British bombers could pitch their heavier Mills grenades. This, too, was true. A third rumour caused great unease. It was said that troops marching up to battle were kept away from soldiers being brought out of action because the sight of these battered victims might damage morale among the fresh troops. And this also was true.

Nevertheless, the Australians, especially the 1st Division, were confident. The men of the 1st had been at Gallipoli and many of them thought that nothing could be as tough as that. They had confidence in their leader, Major General H.B. 'Hooky' Walker. He genuinely cared for his men and he became angry when he thought that his British superiors were putting them into ill-advised actions. They were about to do just that.

A German artillery unit load shells during an attack on Allied positions. Most shells were packed with high explosive and broke into chunks, others were primed to discharge their contents a few metres above the ground showering enemy troops with deadly metal balls.

## POZIÈRES

On the night of 19 July 1916, the 1st Division's leading units marched into the town of Albert (pronounced 'albare'), just behind the front. The men curiously eyed a gilded statue of the Virgin Mary that hung precariously from the spire of the shell-battered cathedral. Eight kilometres from Albert they filed into trenches and fell into an exhausted sleep on the spot.

When they awoke in the morning, the men saw ahead of them a ruined village with the remains of hedges and orchards. 'That's Pozières on the Albert–Bapaume road,' British soldiers told them. Situated on top of a ridge, Pozières was of great tactical value. The Germans knew this and had defended their lines with numerous machine-gun posts. They had also transformed a single two-storey house into an apparently impregnable concrete block with a steel-reinforced tower at one corner. The Australians called it Gibraltar because of its strength.

For the next six weeks the ruined village of Pozières and the fields beyond it would be the scene of the toughest and most costly battle that Australian soldiers have ever endured.

The British had already made four unsuccessful attacks against the German fortifications with the loss of 12 000 men when the AIF 1st Division was ordered to make a night attack on 23 July. Meanwhile, the 2nd Division was brought close up, ready to support the 1st Division. At first, the men of the 2nd were excited as they watched the inferno of shellfire, but they became silent when they realised what hell their mates were enduring.

Under brilliant white flares fired by the watchful Germans, the Australians crept and slithered over the churned-up battlefield, drawing ever closer to the enemy trenches. Some men closed to within 20 metres of them before waiting for the attack to begin. Sweating artillerymen dragged an 18-pounder field gun, its wheels and harness muffled with sacking, to within 200 metres of the trenches: this was virtually point-blank range.

At 28 minutes past midnight, the Diggers seized the front German position as the shelling moved forward. In similar movements, the Australians advanced through the ruins of the village. Using machine-guns, they shot to pieces an entire German battalion making a counter-attack.

In fierce struggles, two Australians, Lieutenant Arthur Blackburn and Private John Leak, displayed outstanding valour. Together, their exploits illustrate the type of sustained fighting during the Somme battles.

Blackburn, with 50 men, was sent to capture a German machine-gun post that was causing casualties and holding up the advance. He made two attacks with four men and on each occasion all four were killed. On a third attempt, Blackburn captured an enemy trench and, in a fourth movement, he gained and held 250 metres of trench. He had not silenced the machine-gun, but he held this great length of trench for seven more hours with only 30 men, relieving the pressure on other units.

Private Leak's exploit was of the do-or-die type for which the Diggers became famous on the Western Front. During his company's assault, the Germans' lighter grenades were outranging the Australians' grenades.

## 'STRETCHER BEARER! STRETCHER BEARER!'

That shout sounded all around the battlefield during the fighting and the bearers never failed to answer the call for help, no matter the danger to their lives.

Unarmed and upright when carrying a wounded man, they constantly risked being hit by bullets and pieces of exploding shell. The Red Cross armband that they wore did not promise protection and many bearers were hit by deliberate sniper fire. Fighting soldiers said that stretcher-bearers working in the open during battle were the real heroes of the war.

Thousands of Diggers volunteered to become bearers, despite the arduous and harrowing work it took to clear the wounded from a battlefield.

The labour was so exhausting that in heavy mud a team of eight bearers and sometimes ten was needed to get a wounded man to an aid post or field ambulance.

Bringing in a wounded man was not merely a matter of getting him off the killing field. He then had to be carried along crowded trenches to an aid post. Stretcher-bearers had no priority of way. Often the only way they could move with their burden was to hold the stretcher high above their heads. They were glad when their charge was unconscious and therefore still because often a wounded man would writhe and scream in pain, making their job more difficult.

The hardest part of the bearers' job came after a major battle, when so many men littered the field that it was not possible to rescue all of them. Then the bearers had the terrible responsibility of deciding which casualties seemed to have the best chance of surviving. Despite their experienced judgment, the bearers often reached the regimental aid post or casualty clearing station with a dead man on the stretcher.

Leak leapt out of his trench, exposing himself to machine-gun fire at close range, and threw three grenades into the enemy bombing post. Then he jumped into the bombing post and bayoneted three unwounded enemy bombers. German reinforcements drove the Australians back from trench to trench and on each occasion, Leak was the last to withdraw, all the time throwing grenades. Faced with his stubborn resistance, the Germans fled. Leak led reinforcements in the recapture of the lost trenches.

Blackburn and Leak were each awarded the Victoria Cross, the army's highest award for bravery.

Angered and frustrated by sniper fire, groups of Australians went looking for Germans in cellars and dugouts and drove them out with phosphorus bombs. As the terrified Germans emerged, the Diggers shot or bayoneted them. Sometimes they gave them a 'sporting chance' to run for their lives — but it was a thin chance.

On the morning of 25 July, the Germans made a strong attempt to recapture part of their trench system. What followed was one of the most intense bomb fights in war history.

One sergeant stripped to the waist in the summer heat and threw bombs for an hour with German grenades bursting around him. One exploded on his chest but he fought on, his body covered with blood, until he dropped with exhaustion.

Other soldiers threw bombs until their arms gave out. During the fight, German snipers shot many Australians, especially those who jumped out of trenches to get a better throw. Using bayonets, bullets and mortars, as well as grenades, the Australians held the key trenches and, after three hours of incessant fighting, the surviving Germans staggered away.

An Australian searches a recently captured German whose friends have already been processed. The Diggers called this activity 'ratting'. Soldiers on both sides usually didn't mind being taken prisoner because it meant an escape from life in the trenches.

In three days of fighting the 1st Division lost 5285 officers and men. The rest were exhausted and the 2nd Division replaced the 1st. Sergeant Edward Rule, who saw the 1st Division move into the rest area, wrote that they 'looked like men who had been in hell, drawn and haggard and so dazed that they appeared to be walking in a dream and their eyes looked glassy and starey'.

The Australians' stubborn fortitude astonished British officers. During the Pozières fighting, a senior British soldier, Brigadier–General Page Croft, came across a blood-spattered Australian sitting in a trench with a bandaged hand and asked what he was doing.

'I'm resting from our bomb fight in Munster Ally,' the soldier replied.

Page Croft told him that in his condition he should be resting in a dressing station.

'But I'm going back to the bomb fight!' the Australian protested.

'You're no good there with a damaged right hand,' the Brigadier pointed out.

'That's all right,' the Digger said cheerfully. 'I'm left-handed.'

Suspecting that he was lying, Page Croft ordered him to remove the bandage and saw that two fingers of his right hand, his throwing hand, had been blown off. In admiration, he shook the Digger's left hand and ordered him to the rear and an advanced dressing station. 'He was a brave man,' the brigadier reported, 'and I fear that he may have returned to the bomb fight by a roundabout route.'

Troops at rest in a captured trench.

As the men of each division became exhausted, the division was withdrawn, the men briefly rested and then put in again. As a result of these attacks, the Australians captured, step by step, the crest of the Pozières ridge.

The Australians made their last attack at Pozières just before dawn on 3 September. Canadian and British troops then took over the fight. On seven occasions the AIF had been used like a battering ram at Pozières and it had lost 23 000 officers and men.

\* \* \*

Active service on the Somme had a depressing effect on the Australian soldiers. After a time, there seemed to be no possibility of survival. A soldier's skill could play only a limited part in bringing him through sustained shellfire or the vicious hail of machine-gun bullets.

Sometimes British generals visited a camp to praise and encourage a unit that had been in battle. Most of these generals did not realise that they were speaking mostly to reinforcements who had just joined the unit and who had little understanding of what the general was talking about. Most of the men to whom the generals were referring in their praise were dead or in hospital with wounds.

Describing the trench warfare, Sergeant Edward Rule wrote, 'We had not gone far before we found that our trench had been blown in. Dead men were lying along it. Some were partly buried with just an arm or a leg sticking out, and it was here that I came to know what the spongy feeling underfoot meant. It was the first time I had ever scrambled over dead and I was more than terrified; I had never before been so horrified in my life. The shelling and the dead, lying in all sorts of attitudes, were enough to send new men mad.'

## BRIEF REST — BACK TO WINTER BATTLE

The Diggers were exhausted and needing rest, so they were withdrawn from the Somme in September 1916 and sent to the Ypres Salient (pronounced 'eepre') in Belgium. They were told that they would be spending winter in the relative quiet of the Salient to reform and reinforce. 'Wipers', the soldiers' name for Ypres, seemed a reasonable place to do this. Even so, there was hard soldiering to do. The British defences were weak and in some places the Germans could have walked through if they had known. Australian raids into no-man's-land prevented the enemy from finding out about the Allied gaps.

New officers were sent to training schools and some Diggers were granted leave in England. Then, on 9 October, came the bombshell the Diggers had been dreading: the 1st, 2nd and 5th divisions were ordered back to the Somme to help break the stalemate. The men were deeply disappointed and angry, and felt they had been betrayed. When told that they were chosen because they were the most determined troops available, they complained that they were being exploited rather than complimented.

The men of the 5th Division, the first to return to the Somme, found to their dismay that winter had also arrived. The battlefield and the rear areas were one vast quagmire, churned into gluey mud by shellfire, supply trucks, guns and wagons, and countless soldiers' boots. It took twelve hours to march the ten kilometres to the front as the men, at each step, had to tug their feet from the clinging mud.

Horses strain to haul an Australian transport wagon through the mud. On the Western Front, horse-drawn wagons were a far more common form of transport than motorised vehicles.

Fighting, always dangerous, was now a nightmare come true. On 5 November 1916 men of the 1st Division were ordered to capture a small enemy salient poking into the British lines near the village of Gueudecourt. The attack was made half an hour after midnight in drenching rain. Caught in the mud, the men reached the front line trench strained and tired. Enemy shrapnel bombardment prevented the units from assembling in no-man's-land, as planned. As support troops reached the already crowded trench, the first arrivals lay across the top of it in great discomfort while the newcomers crawled in below them. And all this happened under fire.

The attack itself began well despite the incessant German flares illuminating the landscape. Under German bombs and bullets, the Diggers' formations then broke up at the German wire. Grim bands of Australians struggled into some enemy positions and killed many Germans. Inevitably, however, they had to retire. The 1st Battalion suffered 170 casualties for no gain at all.

Later that morning, with a full gale in their faces, the 7th Brigade was sent into an attack but the men ran into stronger opposition than expected. Machine-gun fire killed many Australians and pinned down the rest. Their rifles became clogged with mud and hardly a shot could be fired. The 7th Brigade suffered 819 casualties.

Still the British commanders persisted with their lunatic tactics. On 14 November, the 19th, 25th and 28th battalions attacked at Flers. They captured part of their objectives and held them for a few days, but at a cost of 901 casualties, about two-thirds of their strength.

Demanding the inconceivable, the order was given to repeat the attacks at the 'earliest possible moment'. but progress was impossible. General Sir Henry Rawlinson ordered 'a more offensive attitude'. Doggedly,

# RUNNERS — 'I GOT THROUGH, SIR'

Runners were soldiers who had the special job of carrying messages between the front line and battalion headquarters. Men employed as runners for trench or battle duty were among the most rigorously trained specialists in the AIF.

Runners had to go to the battlefront one or two days before the rest of the battalion. This gave them time to learn their way around the mazes of trenches.

Runners carried a compass and were identified by red armbands to indicate that these men were on special duty and could not be put into the firing line. Being a runner was not a safe job, however, as they were frequently exposed to enemy fire and many runners became casualties. In this emergency any reliable soldier might find himself doing a runner's duty in hurrying a message from battalion HQ to the front line or vice versa.

The runners' courage was as legendary as that of the stretcher-bearers. One runner turned up at his brigade HQ, passed on a message and said weakly, 'I got through, sir' and then died from wounds received on his desperate journey. Another runner was hit by pieces of bursting shell. His wounds were mortal and he knew it. He died while lying on his back with the message paper held high between his fingers. Another soldier retrieved it and passed it on.

Of course, when telephone communications worked there was less need to depend on the runners' courage. Under shellfire, however, the lines were often broken.

the Diggers tried even harder to give Rawlinson what he wanted. On 4 February, the order was to capture Stormy Trench north of Gueudecourt. There was no particular tactical advantage in this; Rawlinson merely wanted to 'keep Jerry jumpy' (Jerry and Fritz were nicknames for the Germans). The operation was entrusted to the 13th Battalion, one company of which was led by the much-admired Captain Harry Murray. Eight of his men were due to set off on their London leave on 3 February, but insisted on staying with the company to take part. One man, ill with dysentery, left his bed to go into action.

Each of Murray's 36 bombers had at least 20 grenades, following them were 20 carriers with 24 grenades each. The riflemen, who made up the bulk of the force, carried six grenades, a task made easier because in the intense cold they were all wearing large overcoats with deep pockets.

As they lay in the snow waiting for the attack to begin, the Diggers had a rum issue; it was one of the very few occasions on which Australian soldiers had a drink *before* action. The Australian barrage began at 9.58 pm. Following closely behind their own bursting shells, the infantry were successful in the opening stages. They fought off the Germans with grenades, captured a large section of Stormy Trench and seized 66 prisoners. The German counter artillery barrage then struck the Australians, causing casualties among the stretcher-bearers, the German prisoners and the grenade-carrying parties.

In the trench, Murray had thrown up a barricade of wire, debris and even German bodies to prevent the Germans from rushing along it in a counter-attack. He manned the barricade with his bombers. As the German shelling diminished, enemy soldiers lobbed 20 grenades simultaneously over the barricade. This onslaught broke Murray's bombers and he now had a tremendous fight on his hands.

Cooks of the 27th Battalion escape the horrors of war for a moment. They named their pets 'The Royal Family'. Behind them is a mobile field-kitchen which was used to cook food close to the front.

18

A group of the 22nd Machine Gun Company prepare for the next assault in a hastily built front line trench. The officer at top right is scrutinising the German defences for any gaps or enemy movement.

Encouraging his surviving bombers to hold on, he ordered Private M.D Robertson, who had been badly wounded in the face, to fire rifle grenades beyond the Germans in their part of the trench, thus laying a bomb barrage between them and their supplies. Then he rushed 20 men from another point and fought off German attempts to break down his barricade. An officer of great energy, Murray explored the warren of trenches — a dangerous activity — so that he could anticipate other counter-attacks. He held Stormy Trench until his company was relieved at 8 am next morning, but the 13th Battalion had suffered 233 casualties in what was classified as 'a minor operation'.

Murray was awarded the Victoria Cross.

It is not surprising that in the awful conditions of winter fighting on the Somme, some soldiers, broken and depressed by the dreadful conditions and the appalling things they had seen, became deserters and walked over to the enemy. Some contrived to be taken prisoner so as to hide their desertion, but others slipped away from their own lines, held up a white cloth and gave themselves up. They knew that the front line enemy troops would pass them back to prison camps. No matter how uncomfortable and boring captivity might be, they would be drier and warmer than in the trenches — and safer, too.

A few men took a much more drastic step to escape from their dreadful life. One soldier, told that his already bloodied and suffering battalion was ordered back into the front line, said, 'I'm not going in — I'm finished'. He shot himself dead in front of his mates and they, understanding his desperation, made no effort to stop him. They did not regard him as a coward, but as a brave man.

Haig's tactics of 'wearing down' the enemy had not worked. It was the British and Dominion armies which were worn down. During the First Battle of the Somme they suffered 410 000 casualties to the Germans' 180 000.

# TRENCH LIFE: RATS AS BIG AS CATS

A typical day for the average Digger on the front line was not spent in furious fighting with the enemy. Living for days on end in a hole in the ground, the real enemy was more often boredom, misery and the weather.

Some periods and some sectors were much worse than others. For instance, in the winter of 1916–1917, there were no 'proper' trenches—only weather-eroded, muddy ditches. There was no point in trying to improve the trenches because the mud would collapse them or within hours an enemy bombardment would wreck them.

Some trenches were without barbed wire protection because the soldiers of both sides were incapable of moving, let alone erecting swathes of wire. Wet through from constant drizzle, freezing cold and desperate for a hot meal, the miserable men huddled under whatever shelter they could scratch together. Soldiering was just a matter of surviving until the trench relief troops arrived.

Should an attack have been contemplated, the slimy trench walls prevented the men from climbing out. So did the absence of wooden ladders, which the men burned in an attempt to keep warm. Duckboards, burial crosses and even the hard army biscuits were used for the same purpose.

The Australians and Indians, coming from warmer climates, found the winters unbearable. 'No Australian boy should be expected to live in this dreadful cold,' one soldier wrote home.

According to a lot of soldiers, mud was preferable to ground frozen hard. Many a shell sank into the mud and did not explode, but one that burst on impact on a hard surface sent red-hot shards and splinters in all directions.

The sides of trenches were covered with slugs and horned beetles, but rats were probably the worst horror. Tens of millions of rats lived on the battlefields. They fed on corpses, grew as large as cats and sometimes attacked sleeping men. They spread disease and contaminated food. Experienced Diggers said they could sense shellfire half an hour before it began and they stayed in their holes while the gunfire lasted. Many soldiers were more horrified by these foul creatures than anything else about front line life.

Lice were the constant scourge of every Digger. The tiny insects flourished in the seams of dirty clothing where their eggs were incubated by body heat. Widely known as 'chats' among the Diggers, lice left blotchy and itchy marks all over the body except on the head. Nits infested the men's hair and every company had a barber to shave them to the skull.

On top of all these horrors were the smells. A doctor said of his own regimental aid post, 'There is blood everywhere; all other smells are drowned by its stench. Fumes from a coke brazier fill the place, and bits of clothing, equipment, and dirty bloody dressings.'

One officer estimated that on the battlefield of the First Somme there were 7000 corpses to the square mile. 'Your nose told you where they lay thickest,' he wrote.

Such was life on the Somme, but most books do not reveal its real horrors.

An Australian soldier snatches some sleep in the most comfortable place he can find — he was lucky it was not raining! His rifle is close at hand in case of a surprise attack.

Poison gas was first used as a weapon by the Germans early in the war. Crude gas masks were quickly issued to all front-line soldiers. This type, with eye goggles and box respirator, was one of the better, later versions.

## SECOND BATTLE OF THE SOMME

The AIF fought several major battles in 1917 and throughout the winter of 1917–1918 the Diggers were continually engaged in aggressive patrolling, and they became experts in quick raids on enemy trenches and posts, but most of the men wanted to 'get on with the real war'.

They were not to know that the wily German Chief-of-Staff General Ludendorff and his clever planners were preparing to stoke up the 'real war'. They intended to launch a great fresh Battle of the Somme, as well as attacks elsewhere, as soon as winter ended.

The *Kaiserschlacht*, or Emperor's Battle, began on 21 March 1917. Using force unseen in the war until this time, the German Army broke through the British lines to the south. Ludendorff was steering his troops towards the crucial city of Amiens. In just a few days, the Germans reversed the hard-won Allied gains of the previous year.

Along a front of 80 kilometres, more than 500 000 Germans attacked 160 000 British. From the outset of the battle, large enemy reserves swelled the number of attacking divisions to 64, more than the total number of British divisions on the whole of the Western Front. In all, 1 150 000 German troops were engaged in the tremendous assaults.

Wherever the British resistance was strong the German advance halted, allowing the neighbouring waves to outflank the obstacle on either side and crush it. British troops in the exposed positions were taken by surprise, surrounded and overwhelmed, often before they had realised what had happened.

The situation was critical and an Australian officer in northern France wrote, 'We all have the feeling that if we could only get down there it would be all right'.

On 25 March, the 3rd and 4th Divisions got their wish to be 'down there'. Led by their bands, they headed for the Somme. At one town, even though Australians had not been there before, the people recognised their nationality and began to call excitedly to one another, 'Les Australiens!' Old people already on their way out of the danger zone began to unload their carts. When one Digger asked them why they were doing this, he was told, 'It is now not necessary. You Australians are here'.

The Australians were equally confident; 'The retreat is over,' said a Digger to a French woman as he sat cleaning his rifle while his unit halted on its way to join the battle, 'There are plenty of Australians here now.'

On 27 March the AIF 3rd Division, when taking up positions on the Amiens–Albert road, found that they were the only traffic moving towards the enemy. Streaming past them in the opposite direction were refugees and British soldiers, including heavy artillery. An artillery brigadier said to one Digger officer, 'You Australians think you can do anything, but you haven't a chance of holding the Huns'.

The Australian said, 'Will you stay and support us if we do?' And this the brigadier willingly did.

A British major said, 'The Australians were the first cheerful, stubborn people we had met in the retreat'.

On 4 April the German infantry reached the outskirts of Villers-Bretonneux. The township, which had vital tactical value, seemed as good as lost.

The 36th Battalion, under Lieutenant–Colonel J.A. Milne, had been waiting in a hollow in the town for just such an emergency. Milne led a charge. The Germans, seeing the even line of Australians advancing with their bayonets flashing in the sun, hesitated in disorder. Transfixed by the deadly threat approaching them, they broke ranks and fled back nearly two kilometres to their old trenches.

Australian soldiers on their way to a new sector, share lunch with some curious French children.

23

## 'YOU HAVE ASTONISHED THE WHOLE CONTINENT'

The Australians' finest feat of arms took place at the village of Le Hamel, close to the banks of the Somme, on 4 July 1918. The entire planning was carried out by Lieutenant–General John Monash, who had recently been appointed Commander-in-Chief of all the Australian forces. For the time, Monash's tactics were revolutionary. First, his plans were meticulous in their thoroughness. They covered 454 points and he warned his officers that he would permit no deviation from them. Also, he proposed an all-arms attack, involving artillery, infantry, aircraft and tanks, which were then a new weapon.

Monash could afford only 7 500 men for the Hamel operation and he used four brigades, one each from the 2nd, 3rd, 4th and 5th divisions. In this way all divisions would gain experience from working with the tanks and no one division would have to bear all the losses. Monash also asked for 2 000 Americans, organised in eight companies. The United States had joined the War the previous year and many American troops had been training under Australian guidance.

Monash was given 60 tanks—the massive Mark Vs. At Bullecourt, the previous year, the tanks had failed the Australians in battle and they no longer trusted them. Before Hamel, however, the Tank Corps invited the Diggers to inspect their latest 'monsters' and the curious Australians clambered all over the tanks and went for rides in them. These new tanks could move almost as fast as running infantry and were manoeuvrable. Each company gave a name to the tank allotted to it, such as Eureka, Gloria and Aussie.

Monash ordered that the capture of the German positions at Hamel would take 90 minutes, an extraordinarily short time for battle on the Western Front. British officers thought that he was crazy to commit himself a definite length of time, especially such a short period.

The Germans knew nothing of the imminent attack. The noise of the approaching tanks was screened by artillery fire and bombs dropped from aircraft. The start time was 3.10 am and the Diggers advanced behind the tanks, each of which was marked with the infantry's own battalion colours. The tanks tore holes in the

This damaged Mark V tank was photographed outside Hamel village after the battle. A victorious French flag flies from a rooftop in the background. It was placed there by Major J.T. Moran, 43rd Batallion. Only three of the 60 tanks engaged in the battle were knocked out.

General Monash, Commander-in-Chief of the AIF, presents a decoration to a Digger of the 2nd Division.

barbed wire and enemy bullets simply bounced off their armour. With their greater speed than earlier tanks they lurched across enemy trenches rather than into them and their machine-gunners provided steady covering fire for the infantry.

Some of the tanks were 'carriers' built to transport stores, such as food and water, ammunition, barbed wire and pickets, trenching equipment, sandbags and medical supplies. Gone were the days of struggling men carrying great loads along communication trenches and risking their lives every foot of the way to the front.

Monash also made imaginative use of aircraft. For the first time ammunition was delivered to the Australian troops by parachute, saving infantrymen much hard and dangerous work. The Australian Flying Corps also helped overcome delays in receiving essential battlefield information. Flying no more than 500 feet above ground, two-seater planes carrying a pilot and an observer allowed constant study of the progress of battle. The observer marked on a map the precise movements of Australian infantry, enemy positions and other vital facts. The pilot then flew at top speed to drop the map in a weighted container attached to a multicoloured streamer to a waiting soldier motorcyclist. Monash expected to have the necessary information within ten minutes of its being recorded over the front.

Private Frank Roberts of the 21st Battalion wrote soon after the battle, 'Left support trench at 1.30 am loaded like a mule. Usual fighting order — 220 rounds, two Mills bombs and extra water bottle, shovel down the back and a pannier of ammunition for the Lewis gun — all hellish weighty. Knees knocked when barrage opened but after the start all trepidation vanished. Wonderful barrage put up … we caught glimpses of Fritz going for his life. No return barrage and no machine-gun fire. Met no Fritzes myself until near the final objective. Spared his life to rat him but found nothing.'

Private Roberts was more fortunate than most of his comrades. Elsewhere, the Germans manned many machine-guns and furious fighting took place when the enemy, unlike those seen by Private Roberts, did not 'go for their lives'.

Private Harry Dalziel, from Atherton in Queensland, was a member of the 15th Battalion, whose task it was to capture Pear Trench, one of the Germans' forward positions and the key to their entire defence. Under murderous fire, the Australians' attack came to a complete halt. Single-handedly, and armed only with a revolver, Dalziel charged the enemy gun which was causing the most damage and killed or captured the entire crew. His trigger finger was shot off and he lost much blood, but he made several trips over open ground to collect ammunition for his Lewis machine-gun until he was shot in the head. He survived the wound, was presented with a Victoria Cross and returned home and lived to the age of 72.

The battle was over in 93 minutes instead of 90 but the pleased Monash did not complain about the extra time!

About 2 000 Germans were killed or wounded, and 1 500 taken prisoner. Also captured were two field guns, 32 trench mortars and 177 machine-guns. Only three British tanks were disabled and they were recovered. The total casualties of the attacking infantry were about 1 400, including 176 Americans.

The great Hamel success came while the Supreme War Council was meeting in Paris with its members lamenting that apart from the Australian front there seemed to be little progress against the Germans. The French Prime Minister, Georges Clemenceau, visited the headquarters of the 4th Division to speak to men who had been at Hamel. 'When the Australians came to France, the French people expected a great deal of you,' he said. 'We knew that you would fight a real fight, but we did not know that from the beginning you would astonish the whole continent. I shall return to Paris tomorrow and say to my countrymen, "I have seen the Australians. I have looked in their faces. I know that these men will fight alongside us again until the cause for which we are fighting is safe."'

A Lewis machine-gunner and his mates tensely await the order to attack. On the right a soldier is using a periscope to safely survey no-man's-land

Hamel marked the end, once and for all, of the mainly defensive attitude of the British front and it forced Field Marshal Haig and the senior commanders to examine the possibilities of offensive action following the methods used by General Monash, who was knighted for his services.

A great Allied offensive began one month later, with the Australians spearheading the assault from the trenches they had captured at Hamel. The operation was based on the use of 430 tanks, with Australian, Canadian and British infantry advancing behind them across a broad front.

For the first time in the history of the Australian Corps, all five divisions were involved in what Monash called 'the most important battle operation ever undertaken by the Corps'. The Canadians operated on the Australians' right and two British divisions guarded their left flank.

What would be known as the Battle of Amiens began at 4.20 am on 8 August, some 30 kilometres to the rear of Amiens—the battle was given its name because it marked the end of any German threat against that important city.

The fighting continued along the line of the River Somme and sometimes on its banks. The quality of Australian junior leadership was always evident. Advancing from Villers-Bretonneux, the 28th Battalion moved towards the German defences. The Germans had left a single gap in the barbed wire in hopes that the Australians would funnel through it and be slaughtered in thousands by the machine-guns sited opposite. The 28th Battalion fell into the trap and was stopped cold. Lieutenant Alfred Gaby, a 24-year-old company commander, rushed the German positions. Running along the parapet, oblivious to the murderous fire, he emptied his .45 revolver into the garrison, drove the crews from their guns and forced the surrender of 50 Germans with four machine-guns. Rapidly re-organising his men, he led them on to his company's final objective. A few days later Gaby was shot dead by a sniper while again directing his men under fire. He was one of the several Diggers to be awarded the Victoria Cross during the Second Battle of the Somme.

The Second Battle of the Somme can be said to have ended on 1 September 1918 with the capture of the Germans' major fortifications on the Somme. One was Péronne, which sat astride the river, and the other Mont St Quentin, which overlooked the town. The award of seven Victoria Crosses during the period 28 August–1 September demonstrates the quality of the Australians' heroism in these actions.

During the fighting at Mont St Quentin and Péronne, the Diggers attacked more than their number of Germans in strong positions and captured more of them than they could safely hold. Elements of three pathetically weakened Australian divisions dealt a staggering blow to five German divisions, including two elite ones. It was a wholly AIF planned and executed battle.

The Second Battle of the Somme was a turning point for the Allies, especially the Australian victories at Villers-Bretonneux and Le Hamel. The relatively small battle of Le Hamel had big results. It showed the Allied High Command that there was a new way of attacking the Germans and winning, rather than going on as before and launching an old-fashioned offensive and losing Allied lives by the hundreds of thousands.

What had started as a ferocious attack by the Germans in the spring of 1918 was successfully countered, and was then turned around in the summer.

Now the end of the war and an Allied victory before winter seemed possible. This indeed happened. On 11 November 1918, World War I ended, with Germany and her allies defeated.

A Sydney mother is ruinited with her son, returned wounded from the war. To have a son, husband or brother return safely, even if badly hurt, was the ardent wish of every family.

15 000 Australians died fighting in the two battles of The Somme; some 60 000 died over the course of the entire war. This was a terrible blow for a young country such as Australia. There were few families who were not touched in some way by tragedy and expressions of community grief can be seen in the war memorials found in towns and suburbs all across Australia.

Today, the dreadful battlefields have returned to peaceful farmland. Apart from the many memorials to the dead, there are few reminders of what happened there long ago. The deep trenches have mostly disappeared and the towns and villages reduced to flattened rubble have been rebuilt.

There are still some old Diggers who remember the fighting on the Somme, but their ranks grow thinner each year. They are far outnumbered by the white headstones over the graves of their mates who lie in one or other of about 800 cemeteries in France and Belgium. Many are beautiful garden cemeteries maintained by the Commonwealth War Graves Commission. Three thousand Diggers who died of wounds or disease are buried in 430 cemeteries in Britain.

For so many Australians, the road to the Somme—and to other battlefields of the Western Front—was a dead end.

# Glossary

AID POST A medical station close to the fighting staffed by doctors and soldiers trained in first aid. It was the first port of call for the sick or wounded.

AIF The Australian Imperial Force, the all-volunteer Australian Army of 1914–1918.

ALLIES The collective name given to the nations fighting the 'Central Powers' of Germany, Austria-Hungary, Bulgaria and the Ottoman Empire (Turkey). Britain, France, Russia and Italy were the principal Allies. The United States fought with the allies after 1917.

ARTILLERY Heavy guns used in land warfare. They may be fixed or mobile, but are too large to be carried by an individual soldier.

ATTRITION A war of attrition is one of sustained pressure intended to wear out the strength of the opponent. The aim is to create losses of personnel and material which cannot be replaced.

BAYONET A short sword fitted to the end of a rifle. Bayonets were used in close fighting with the enemy and were meant to terrify them.

CASUALTIES Soldiers killed, wounded, ill, taken prisoner or 'missing'.

DEFENSIVE/OFFENSIVE A defensive attitude in war is to concentrate on holding positions and repelling the enemy. Offensive is to go on the attack.

DUCKBOARD Walkway made of wooden slats to provide solid footing on wet, muddy ground.

DUGOUT A living space dug into the ground or into the side of a trench as protection from shell fire and the weather.

INFANTRY The foot soldiers, armed with rifles, machine-guns, mortars and grenades. The infantry did the actual close-quarter fighting.

LEAVE A break away from army duty; sometimes only for a few hours. Australians on longer breaks often went to England, Paris or a pleasant town well away from the fighting.

NO-MAN'S-LAND The area between the two opposing front lines.

OFFICER Any soldier with a rank of Second Lieutenant or above. Depending on their seniority, officers were paid more and they had many more responsibilities than their men. About one in 30 soldiers of the AIF was an officer.

PHOSPHOROUS BOMB A grenade which, on exploding, everything around it alight, including enemy soldiers.

RIFLE GRENADES By attaching a steel cup to the rifle barrel and using a special cartridge full of a propellant charge known as ballastite, a grenade could be fired 150 metres. By hand, a grenade could be lobbed only 20 metres.

SALIENT A section of the front line which bulged into the enemy's front line. A salient was vulnerable to attack from three sides and nearly always resulted in heavy casualties to the troops holding it.

SNIPER A highly trained rifleman who picked off enemy soldiers one by one; a crack shot.

STALEMATE A standstill where neither side can advance against the other.

TOMMY A nickname for a British soldiers. As Australians were known as 'Digger', Germans as 'Fritz' so the British were known as 'Tommy'. Thomas Atkins was a name used as an example on British Army forms early in the nineteenth century.

VICTORIA CROSS (VC) The highest award for individual acts of bravery in the British and Dominion armies; named after Queen Victoria who created the decoration in the 1850s. It is rarely bestowed.

## Author's Note

I have spent much of my life on Australian battlefields. I can say that the Somme, one of the most important of our campaigning areas, is also one of the most interesting for modern visitors. More and more Australians are making pilgrimages to the Western Front and the Australian memorials to be found there. A magnificent statue and a great new memorial were unveiled in 1998. I wish that all Australians could visit the lands where more than 50 000 young Australians were killed. I must thank the Imperial War Museum, London, and the Australian War Memorial, Canberra, for some of the photographs used in this book. My thanks to Anny De Decker for her work on the typescript.

*   *   *

The book is dedicated to my parents, both of whom served in the Australian Imperial Force on the Somme— Staff Nurse Nellie Pike and Lieutenant Charles Laffin, an infantry officer.

First published in Australia in 1999 by Kangaroo Press
an imprint of Simon & Schuster (Australia) Pty Ltd
20 Barcoo Street, East Roseville NSW 2069

A Viacom Company
Sydney  New York  London  Toronto  Tokyo  Singapore

© John Laffin 1999

All rights reserved. No part of this publication may be reproduced,
stored in a retrieval system, or transmitted, in any form or by any
means, electronic, mechanical, photocopying, recording or otherwise,
without the prior permission of the publisher in writing.

National Library of Australia
Cataloguing-in-Publication data

Laffin, John. 1922-
The Somme
ISBN 0 86417 971 5
1. World War, 1914-1918 – Campaigns – France – Juvenile literature.  2. World War, 1914-1918 – Participation, Australian – Juvenile literature. I. Nathaniel, Errol. II. Title.
940.4272

Set in Times New Roman 12/16
Printed in Hong Kong through Colorcraft

10 9 8 7 6 5 4 3 2 1